Same-Sex Wedding Should I Attend?

A Wise Way to Develop Your Own Response

Other books and studies by **BRUCE B. MILLER**

the WISDOM™
SERIES

Sexuality
Approaching Controversial Issues with
Grace, Truth and Hope

Big God in a Chaotic World
A Fresh Look at Daniel

When God Makes No Sense
A Fresh Look at Habakkuk

Never the Same
A Fresh Look at the Sermon on the Mount

૭◦ఴ

Same-Sex Marriage
A Bold Call to the Church
in Response to the Supreme Court's Decision

Your Church in Rhythm

Your Life in Rhythm
and
Your Life in Rhythm Study Guide

The Leadership Baton
and
The Leadership Baton Group Study Guide
written with Rowland Forman and Jeff Jones

Same-Sex Wedding
Should I Attend?

A Wise Way to Develop
Your Own Response

BRUCE B. MILLER

Dadlin Media
wisdom for life
McKinney, Texas

Dadlin Media is the publishing ministry of Dadlin ministries, an organization committed to helping people develop wisdom for life.

For more information please go to: http://BruceBMiller.com.

ISBN-10: 1-68316-009-6
ISBN-13: 978-1-68316-009-0

Printed in the United States of America
Unless otherwise noted, Scripture taken from the HOLY BIBLE, NEW INTERNATIONAL VERSION. Copyright © 1973, 1978, 1984, 2010.
International Bible Society.
Used by permission of Zondervan Publishing House.

Dadlin Media
—— *wisdom for life* ——
McKinney, TX 75070
BruceBMiller.com

Contents

Introduction

Sarah asked if we could meet privately. As one of the younger ladies on our church staff, she had never asked to meet with me so I sensed it was important. It was. Her sister had just announced her engagement to her same-sex partner. Since Sarah was really close to her older sister, she was pretty sure her sister was going to invite her to be a bridesmaid. She asked me what she should do.

How would you have advised her? What questions should she ask?

Following the SCOTUS *Obergefell v. Hodges* same-sex marriage decision on June 26, 2015, these questions have become more frequent. Bible-believing Christians disagree on how to respond to an invitation to a same-sex wedding. Some say you should attend and others say that you certainly should not attend, and both quote Scripture.

This study is designed to help you, your family, and your team or group, think through the issue biblically and practically. Rather than arguing for any one particular point of view, this study helps you think through the issue yourself.

Using the powerful WISDOM Process© you will work your way through the issue looking at multiple dimensions involved. The "attend-the-wedding-or-not" question raises issues not only about homosexuality, but also about the nature of marriage and of weddings, which are not the same thing. Multiple biblical principles come into play.

How to best benefit from this book

I encourage you to read the following brief summary of The WISDOM Process© because understanding how it works will accelerate and deepen your decision process. You can read "More on The WISDOM Process©" beginning on page 89 and also involve others with you in the study. We learn more and see more when we engage with others in the back and forth of dynamic dialog among a small group.

As you walk through The WISDOM Process© spend significant time working the issue and investigating the Scripture before you seek other counsel by reading the articles. Before you meet as a group to openly discuss the issue, take time to develop your own response and write it down. This will make the discussion richer. (You can benefit from reading the book without talking about it in a group.)

May the Holy Spirit lead you to God-honoring, Christ-centered spiritual wisdom in how you respond to same-sex wedding invitations.

The WISDOM Process©

As children of God living in a hostile world, we need to learn how to think like Christ with biblical, spiritual wisdom for life.

Tested by thousands of people and hundreds of groups, the six-step WISDOM Process© offers a surprisingly simple and profoundly powerful way to think. Today we are drowning in data and starving for wisdom. We Google for information on any topic, but we cannot find wisdom for life's complex challenges. The WISDOM Process helps us move from knowing facts to transforming our lives in God's power. Most adults learn differently than children.

Research into adult learning and studies of ancient education both show that people learn best when they have a reason to learn: a question to answer, a problem to solve or a mystery to unravel. All of us have these in our lives.

⌘ For more on The WISDOM Process© see page 89.

✝ Pray

W **Work the issue:** *What's really at stake?*

I **Investigate Scripture:** *What does God say?*

S **Seek counsel:** *What do wise people say?*

D **Develop your response:** *What do I think?*

O **Openly discuss:** *What do we think?*

M **Move to action:** *What will I do?*

Same-Sex Wedding: Should I Attend?

W Work the issue: *What's really at stake?*

Framing this issue well requires looking through multiple windows. In working through the issue, look through the following windows and any others you can identify.

Morality

What is the faith of the person(s) involved? Are both people Christians? Is only one a Christian, neither, or are you not sure? Is it biblically acceptable for a Christian same-sex couple to marry? What about for a non-Christian couple? Could this be a parallel to the Romans 14 issue of food offered to idols, on which Christians can agree to disagree?

Marriage

What is the nature of marriage biblically? Is it a sacred institution? Is it only between a man and woman for a lifetime, or could it be between any two people who truly love each other? Could the marriage be a civil union recognized by the government rather than a religious union sanctified by God?

Relationship

Is the person getting married a family member, a close friend, a business associate, your boss, co-worker, major client or are they merely an acquaintance? How long have you known them?

Motive

Look into your heart to prayerfully discern your motives. Are you driven more by your desire to show love? To draw your friend to Christ? To avoid approving what you see as sin? Anger? Revulsion? Are you simply uncomfortable? Do you feel pressured by

societal norms? Perhaps you are pressured by your concern over what others might think if you attend, or conversely if you refuse to attend.

Context of the ceremony

Is the wedding a religious sacrament before God or a secular, civil ceremony? Where will the wedding be held? In a church or in a neutral setting such as a courtroom or garden? Will the wedding be conducted by a pastor or by a non-religious person such as a judge?

Cultural meaning

Given the kind of wedding and the nature of your relationship, what will your attendance convey? Are you endorsing the marriage or simply supporting the person? In general, what does attending a wedding communicate in your cultural context? How does it compare to a non-Christian attending a Christian baptism? How would you compare or contrast attending a same-sex wedding with the wedding of a couple who is getting married only because the woman is pregnant, or because they are too young, or have known each other a very short time? Does the size of the wedding matter, several hundred versus merely dozens of attendees?

Biblical principles

Which biblical principles should guide your decision? Are some principles more important than others? How do you weigh standing for righteousness over acting in love? How do you weigh endorsing an action you oppose against expressing hospitality to people you love? What does the gospel imply for how we should respond?

Courses of action

There are far more options and variables than simply attending or not attending the wedding. For instance, will you give a gift? Make a toast? Be in the wedding party if

asked? Go to the reception only? If you are qualified, would you perform the ceremony? As a father, would you walk your daughter down the aisle? What about sending a note of congratulations? Could you have a conversation in advance with your family member or friend who is getting married, empowering them to decide whether they really want you there or not, given that you disapprove of the wedding?

❖ As you see it, what is the central issue before us?

█ Investigate Scripture: *What does God say?*

Because our issue involves a range of topics, we will need to consider quite a few passages to hear what God has to say. We will explore passages on homosexuality, marriage, weddings, debatable matters, and ones with broader principles that could guide this kind of decision.

Passages on Homosexuality

A total of seven biblical passages speak directly to homo-sexuality. It all starts with creation where we see that God created one man and one woman to form a one-flesh bond and multiply. In the Old Testament, four passages directly address same-sex issues: Two stories, one in Genesis 19 with a parallel in Judges 19, and two similar laws in Leviticus 18:22 and 20:13. Genesis 19 tells the infamous story of Sodom where rape of

men and women was threatened. The primary issue was sexual immorality and perversion (Jude 9) as well as arrogance and injustice (Ezekiel 16:49). The laws in Leviticus forbid an array of sexual sin including incest, adultery, bestiality and homo-sexuality. While sacrificial laws do not directly apply today since they are fulfilled in Christ, moral commands repeated in the New Testament do apply directly.

Three passages in the New Testament mention same-sex behavior. The core passage is Romans 1. In context, Paul is giving an illustration of humanity turning from the Creator to the creation. The lustful, unnatural sex of men with men and women with women is itself a consequence of sin. Paul's use of the term "unnatural" echoes the creation order in Genesis. In the next chapter (Romans 2), Paul flips the table by including in God's condemnation those who self-righteously judge people. Paul argues that all people are sinners in need of God's grace. We must read these opening few chapters of Romans in light of the whole book, which is a celebration of God's amazing grace in Jesus available to all of us. The two remaining passages, 1 Corinthians 6 and 1 Timothy 1, put intimate homosexual behavior in lists with other sins.

Creation

Genesis 1:27–28

> *So God created mankind in his own image,*
> *in the image of God he created them;*
> *male and female he created them.*
> *God blessed them and said to them,*
> *"Be fruitful and increase in number; fill the earth and subdue it. Rule over the fish in the sea and the birds in the sky and over every living creature that moves on the ground."*

Genesis 2:18–24

The LORD God said, "It is not good for the man to be alone. I will make a helper suitable for him."

Now the LORD God had formed out of the ground all the wild animals and all the birds in the sky. He brought them to the man to see what he would name them; and whatever the man called each living creature, that was its name. So the man gave names to all the livestock, the birds in the sky and all the wild animals.

But for Adam no suitable helper was found. So the LORD God caused the man to fall into a deep sleep; and while he was sleeping, he took one of the man's ribs and then closed up the place with flesh. Then the LORD God made a woman from the rib he had taken out of the man, and he brought her to the man.

> The man said,
> "This is now bone of my bones
> and flesh of my flesh;
> she shall be called 'woman,'
> for she was taken out of man."
> That is why a man leaves his
> father and mother and is united to
> his wife, and they become one flesh.

Matthew 19:4–6

> "Haven't you read," he replied,
> "that at the beginning the Creator
> 'made them male and female,' and
> said, 'For this reason a man will
> leave his father and mother and be
> united to his wife, and the two will
> become one flesh'? So they are no
> longer two, but one flesh. Therefore
> what God has joined together, let no
> one separate."

Old Testament

Leviticus 18:22

Do not have sexual relations with a man as one does with a woman; that is detestable.

Leviticus 20:13

If a man has sexual relations with a man as one does with a woman, both of them have done what is detestable. They are to be put to death; their blood will be on their own heads.

Genesis 19:1–10

The two angels arrived at Sodom in the evening, and Lot was sitting in the gateway of the city. When he saw them, he got up to meet them and bowed down with his face to the ground. "My lords," he said, "please turn aside to your servant's house. You can wash your feet and spend the night and then go on your way early in the morning."

"No," they answered, "we will spend the night in the square."

But he insisted so strongly that they did go with him and entered his house. He prepared a meal for them, baking bread without yeast, and they ate. Before they had gone to bed, all the men from every part of the city of Sodom—both young and old— surrounded the house. They called to Lot, "Where are the men who came to you tonight? Bring them out to us so that we can have sex with them."

Lot went outside to meet them and shut the door behind him and said, "No, my friends. Don't

do this wicked thing. Look, I have two daughters who have never slept with a man. Let me bring them out to you, and you can do what you like with them. But don't do anything to these men, for they have come under the protection of my roof."

"Get out of our way," they replied. "This fellow came here as a foreigner, and now he wants to play the judge! We'll treat you worse than them." They kept bringing pressure on Lot and moved forward to break down the door.

But the men inside reached out and pulled Lot back into the house and shut the door.

See the parallel story in Judges 19:16–26

While they were enjoying themselves, some of the wicked men

of the city surrounded the house.
Pounding on the door, they shouted
to the old man who owned the
house, "Bring out the man who
came to your house so we can have
sex with him."

New Testament

Romans 1:18–32

The wrath of God is being
revealed from heaven against all
the godlessness and wickedness of
people, who suppress the truth by
their wickedness, since what may be
known about God is plain to them,
because God has made it plain to
them. For since the creation of the
world God's invisible qualities—his
eternal power and divine nature—
have been clearly seen, being
understood from what has been

made, so that people are without
excuse.

For although they knew God,
they neither glorified him as God
nor gave thanks to him, but their
thinking became futile and their
foolish hearts were darkened.
Although they claimed to be wise,
they became fools and exchanged
the glory of the immortal God for
images made to look like a mortal
human being and birds and animals
and reptiles.

Therefore God gave them over
in the sinful desires of their hearts
to sexual impurity for the
degrading of their bodies with one
another. They exchanged the truth
about God for a lie, and worshiped
and served created things rather
than the Creator—who is forever
praised. Amen.

Because of this, God gave them over to shameful lusts. Even their women exchanged natural sexual relations for unnatural ones. In the same way the men also abandoned natural relations with women and were inflamed with lust for one another. Men committed shameful acts with other men, and received in themselves the due penalty for their error.

Furthermore, just as they did not think it worthwhile to retain the knowledge of God, so God gave them over to a depraved mind, so that they do what ought not to be done. They have become filled with every kind of wickedness, evil, greed and depravity. They are full of envy, murder, strife, deceit and malice. They are gossips, slanderers, God-haters, insolent, arrogant and

boastful; they invent ways of doing
evil; they disobey their parents; they
have no understanding, no fidelity,
no love, no mercy. Although they
know God's righteous decree that
those who do such things deserve
death, they not only continue to do
these very things but also approve
of those who practice them.

1 Corinthians 6:9–11

Or do you not know that
wrongdoers will not inherit the
kingdom of God? Do not be
deceived: Neither the sexually
immoral nor idolaters nor
adulterers nor men who have sex
with men nor thieves nor the greedy
nor drunkards nor slanderers nor
swindlers will inherit the kingdom
of God. And that is what some of you
were. But you were washed, you
were sanctified, you were justified

*in the name of the Lord Jesus Christ
and by the Spirit of our God.*

1 Timothy 1:8–11

*We know that the law is good
if one uses it properly. We also
know that the law is made not for
the righteous but for lawbreakers
and rebels, the ungodly and sinful,
the unholy and irreligious, for those
who kill their fathers or mothers,
for murderers, for the sexually
immoral, for those practicing
homosexuality, for slave traders
and liars and perjurers—and for
whatever else is contrary to the
sound doctrine that conforms to the
gospel concerning the glory of the
blessed God, which he entrusted to
me.*

❖ Summarize God's view of same-sex intimacy.

Passages on Marriage

Genesis 2:18

God made marriage. God said,

It is not good for the man to be alone
[so he made a] *helper suitable for him.*

Genesis 2:23

When Adam saw Eve, he spoke the first poetry,

> *This is now bone of my bones and*
> *flesh of my flesh; she shall be called*
> *'woman,' for she was taken out of man.*

Genesis 2:24–25

The Bible then affirms,

> *That is why a man leaves his father*
> *and mother and is united to his wife, and*
> *they become one flesh. Adam and his wife*
> *were both naked, and they felt no shame.*

God told the original couple to be fruitful and multiply, implying in this first command that procreation is an important aspect of marriage.

Jesus affirms creation theology of marriage as one man and one woman for life.

> *"Haven't you read," he replied,*
> *"that at the beginning the Creator*
> *'made them male and female,' and*
> *said, 'For this reason a man will*
> *leave his father and mother and be*

united to his wife, and the two will
become one flesh'? So they are no
longer two, but one flesh. Therefore
what God has joined together, let no
one separate" (Matthew 19:4–6).

Marriage is a picture of God's relationship with Israel and Christ's relationship with the church (Ephesians 5:29–32). And God tells us to keep marriage sacred,

Marriage should be honored by all,
and the marriage bed kept pure, for God
will judge the adulterer and all the sexually
immoral (Hebrews 13:40).

❖   Describe God's view of marriage.

Passages on Weddings

Greek and Hebrew terms for "wedding" are rare in the Bible. There is little theology or biblical guidance on weddings themselves. The following are a few fleeting depictions of weddings but there are no prescriptive passages directing how a couple should conduct a wedding or what it means.

According to Christian ethicist Lewis B. Smedes:

"Myriads of splendid marriages have begun without anything like what we would recognize as a wedding in our culture. And who knows how many weddings have legalized sham marriages?

"The Bible has a lot to say about marriage, but it has little or nothing to say about how marriages must begin. There is a theology of marriage, but there is no divine morality of weddings. Marriage is an invention of God; weddings are inventions of cultures. So when we ask why young people ought to 'get married,' we are asking why they should submit to a cultural custom that changes as culture changes. We will have to put up with an answer that carries less weight than divine law."[1]

Isaac and Rebekah
Genesis 24:67

Isaac brought her into the tent of his mother Sarah, and he married Rebekah. So she became his wife, and he loved her; and Isaac was comforted after his mother's death.

Jacob and Leah
Genesis 29:21–23

Then Jacob said to Laban, "Give me my wife. My time is completed, and I want to make love to her."

So Laban brought together all the people of the place and gave a feast. But when evening came, he took his daughter Leah and brought her to Jacob, and Jacob made love to her.

Implied wedding of Samson to Philistine woman in Judges 14

Scan Judges 14. We see few clues to what was involved, but we can assume his parents attended the wedding since they got the woman for him.

Boaz and Ruth
Ruth 4:9–11

> Boaz said to the elders and all the people, "You are witnesses today that I am buying from Naomi everything that belonged to Elimelech, Chilion, and Mahlon. I will also acquire Ruth the Moabitess, Mahlon's widow, as my wife, to perpetuate the deceased man's name on his property, so that his name will not disappear among his relatives or from the gate of his home. You are witnesses today."
>
> The elders and all the people who were at the gate said, "We are

witnesses. May the LORD make the woman who is entering your house like Rachel and Leah, who together built the house of Israel. May you be powerful in Ephrathah and famous in Bethlehem.

Implied wedding of Esther to Xerxes
Esther 2:17–18

Now the king was attracted to Esther more than to any of the other women, and she won his favor and approval more than any of the other virgins. So he set a royal crown on her head and made her queen instead of Vashti. And the king gave a great banquet, Esther's banquet, for all his nobles and officials. He proclaimed a holiday throughout the provinces and distributed gifts with royal liberality.

A wedding is referred to in the Song of Solomon

Scan Song of Solomon for poetry referring to a wedding in 3:6–5:1.

A wedding song
Psalm 45:14–15

In embroidered garments she is
led to the king;

her virgin companions follow
her—

those brought to be with her.
Led in with joy and gladness,
they enter the palace of the
king.

Jesus at the wedding in Cana
John 2:1–10

On the third day a wedding
took place at Cana in Galilee. Jesus'
mother was there, and Jesus and his
disciples had also been invited to
the wedding. When the wine was

gone, Jesus' mother said to him, "They have no more wine."

"Woman, why do you involve me?" Jesus replied. "My hour has not yet come."

His mother said to the servants, "Do whatever he tells you."

Nearby stood six stone water jars, the kind used by the Jews for ceremonial washing, each holding from twenty to thirty gallons.

Jesus said to the servants, "Fill the jars with water"; so they filled them to the brim.

Then he told them, "Now draw some out and take it to the master of the banquet."

They did so, and the master of the banquet tasted the water that had been turned into wine. He did not realize where it had come from, though the servants who had drawn

the water knew. Then he called the
bridegroom aside and said,
"Everyone brings out the choice
wine first and then the cheaper
wine after the guests have had too
much to drink; but you have saved
the best till now."

The kingdom of heaven is like a wedding banquet
Matthew 22:1–14

Jesus spoke to them again in
parables, saying: "The kingdom of
heaven is like a king who prepared
a wedding banquet for his son."

See the rest of the story in
Matthew 22:3–14. Compare this
passage with the ten virgins with oil
lamps waiting for the bridegroom in
Matthew 25:1–13, and the return of
Jesus to be celebrated as the wedding

of the lamb to her bride in a wedding
supper in Revelation 19:7–9.

> ❖ Summarize insights into weddings
> depicted in the Bible. What was
> involved? Who attended?

Passage on Debatable Matters

Romans 14:1–23

*Accept the one whose faith is
weak, without quarreling over
disputable matters. One person's
faith allows them to eat anything,
but another, whose faith is weak,
eats only vegetables. The one who*

*eats everything must not treat with
contempt the one who does not, and
the one who does not eat everything
must not judge the one who does,
for God has accepted them. Who are
you to judge someone else's
servant? To their own master,
servants stand or fall. And they will
stand, for the Lord is able to make
them stand.*

*One person considers one day
more sacred than another; another
considers every day alike. Each of
them should be fully convinced in
their own mind. Whoever regards
one day as special does so to the
Lord. Whoever eats meat does so to
the Lord, for they give thanks to
God; and whoever abstains does so
to the Lord and gives thanks to God.
For none of us lives for ourselves
alone, and none of us dies for*

ourselves alone. If we live, we live for the Lord; and if we die, we die for the Lord. So, whether we live or die, we belong to the Lord. For this very reason, Christ died and returned to life so that he might be the Lord of both the dead and the living.

You, then, why do you judge your brother or sister? Or why do you treat them with contempt? For we will all stand before God's judgment seat. It is written:

"'As surely as I live,' says the Lord,

'every knee will bow before me;

every tongue will acknowledge God.'"

So then, each of us will give an account of ourselves to God.

Therefore let us stop passing judgment on one another. Instead, make up your mind not to put any stumbling block or obstacle in the way of a brother or sister. I am convinced, being fully persuaded in the Lord Jesus, that nothing is unclean in itself. But if anyone regards something as unclean, then for that person it is unclean. If your brother or sister is distressed because of what you eat, you are no longer acting in love. Do not by your eating destroy someone for whom Christ died. Therefore do not let what you know is good be spoken of as evil. For the kingdom of God is not a matter of eating and drinking, but of righteousness, peace and joy in the Holy Spirit, because anyone who serves Christ in this way is

pleasing to God and receives human approval.

Let us therefore make every effort to do what leads to peace and to mutual edification. Do not destroy the work of God for the sake of food. All food is clean, but it is wrong for a person to eat anything that causes someone else to stumble. It is better not to eat meat or drink wine or to do anything else that will cause your brother or sister to fall.

So whatever you believe about these things keep between yourself and God. Blessed is the one who does not condemn himself by what he approves. But whoever has doubts is condemned if they eat, because their eating is not from faith; and everything that does not come from faith is sin.

❖ How is attending a same-sex
wedding like and unlike eating food
offered to idols?

Passages that Could Guide
Decisions on Debatable Matters

Matthew 7:3

*Why do you look at the speck
of sawdust in your brother's eye and
pay no attention to the plank in
your own eye?*

Luke 15:1–2, Example of Jesus

Now the tax collectors and sinners were all gathering around to hear Jesus. But the Pharisees and the teachers of the law muttered, "This man welcomes sinners and eats with them."

1 Corinthians 5:12–13

What business is it of mine to judge those outside the church? Are you not to judge those inside? God will judge those outside. "Expel the wicked person from among you."

1 Corinthians 9:22

To the weak I became weak, to win the weak. I have become all things to all people so that by all possible means I might save some.

Galatians 6:1–4

Brothers and sisters, if someone is caught in a sin, you who live by the Spirit should restore that person gently. But watch yourselves, or you also may be tempted. Carry each other's burdens, and in this way you will fulfill the law of Christ. If anyone thinks they are something when they are not, they deceive themselves. Each one should test their own actions. Then they can take pride in themselves alone, without comparing themselves to someone else.

Ephesians 5:8–11

For you were once darkness, but now you are light in the Lord. Live as children of light (for the fruit of the light consists in all goodness, righteousness and truth)

*and find out what pleases the Lord.
Have nothing to do with the
fruitless deeds of darkness, but
rather expose them.*

Colossians 4:5–6

*Be wise in the way you act
toward outsiders; make the most of
every opportunity. Let your
conversation be always full of grace,
seasoned with salt, so that you may
know how to answer everyone.*

1 Peter 4:8

*Above all, love each other
deeply, because love covers over a
multitude of sins.*

❖ What principles do you find in these passages that could shed light on the question before us about attending a same-sex wedding?

S Seek counsel: *What do wise people say?*

Choose to read the articles that would be most helpful for you and your group from the following authors. Each author provides wise but differing counsel on our question. All of the articles are reprinted (with permission) on the pages that follow this summary.

Article 1—*Same-Sex Marriage (Thoughtful Response): A Thoughtful Approach to God's Design for Marriage* by Sean McDowell and John Stonestreet (see Barr, et.al. for a similar view) beginning on page 47.

Article 2—*Loving My (LGBT) Neighbor: Being Friends in Grace and Truth* by Glenn Stanton beginning on page 51.

Article 3—*Question: "Should a Christian attend the wedding of a gay couple?"* byCrosswalk.com beginning on page 61.

Article 4 —*Should I Attend the Wedding of a Gay Friend or Family Member?* [Four Views]

ByPeter Ould, Eve Tushnet, Lisa Severine Nolland, Sherif Girgis beginning on page 67.

Article 5—*Attend Your Child's Same-sex Wedding Ceremony* by the National Association of Evangelicals beginning on page 83.

D Develop your response: *What do I think*?

❖ In general, how would you respond to an invitation to attend a same-sex wedding? What biblical truths guide you?

❖ What will you do with a specific invitation you have received (if you have one now, or anticipate one coming)?

⊙ Openly discuss: *What do we think?*

1. How do you biblically evaluate the rightness or wrongness of same-sex marriage regardless of its legal status in a given country?

2. Is same-sex marriage between two Christians analogous to eating food offered to idols (Romans 14)? Why or why not?

3. How do you summarize descriptions of weddings in the Bible in terms of the nature of the ceremonies and who

attended them? What does a wedding signify? What does attending a wedding convey in your culture today?

4. Should any of the following factors influence how you respond to an invitation to a same-sex wedding? How so? And why?
   a. Whether the person(s) getting married is/are Christian(s) or not?
   b. Your relationship to the person(s) such as if they are close family?
   c. The context of the ceremony such as if it is in a church or a park?

5. How do the principles of standing for righteousness and the sacredness of marriage impact how you might respond to an invitation to a same-sex wedding? (Ephesians 5:8–13).

6. If the person(s) getting married is/are not Christian(s), how does the gospel guide our response? Consider 1 Corinthians 5:12–13, 9:22, and Colossians 4:5.

7. If the person(s) getting married is/are Christian(s,) how does love guide us? Consider Matthew 7:3; 1 Peter 4:8, and Galatians 6:1–4.

8. In general, how will you respond to an invitation to a same-sex wedding and why? If you have an invitation before you right now, how will you respond to that specific invitation?

9. Before God, is there room for Christians to differ in their response to invitations to same-sex weddings or is there a biblical response we should all follow?

M **Move to action:** *What will I do?*

❖ Write down how you will respond when
   you are invited to a same-sex wedding
   and why.

❖ If you are married, talk over your decision
   with your spouse.

❖ Take time to have a conversation with the
   person in your life who has invited you to
   their wedding, being sure to listen to
   them deeply, and to assure them of your
   love.

Article 1

Same-Sex Marriage (Thoughtful Response): A Thoughtful Approach to God's Design for Marriage[2]

Sean McDowell and John Stonestreet

What if I'm invited to a same-sex wedding ceremony?

We believe wedding ceremonies are sacred and that attendance implies a complicit blessing of the union itself. At a wedding, a covenant, even when not acknowledged, is being made between two people, the community and God. Therefore, we could not attend a same-sex wedding in good conscience (would we really want to "speak now or forever hold our peace" on this?).

On the other hand, a protest is rarely necessary or helpful. The extent to which Christians should verbally express disagreement will depend on how close we are to those who invite us. It may be appropriate to sit down and calmly explain our disagreement in love, but two things should already be in place. First, there should be a strong relationship. Second, as much as is possible, people should already know where we stand. It's much easier to say, "You know, I think you already know my convictions on gay relationships, so it's probably not a surprise that I cannot come to your ceremony. May we talk about this further?"

It may be that some Christians who share our convictions about marriage will choose to attend a same-sex ceremony. That is a matter of conscience. Others may choose to avoid the ceremony but join the reception and bring a gift. Others may send a gift but avoid the ceremony and reception altogether. Whatever we decide, we must act with a clear conscience before God in good faith. Realize that other Christians, in particular young Christians, will learn from our example.

Article condensed and used by permission.

Article 2

Loving My (LGBT) Neighbor:
Being Friends in Grace and Truth[3]
Glenn T. Stanton

What about a Wedding?

Regardless of whether you live in a state that has legalized same-sex weddings or not, the invitation to such a wedding is something that more are having to face. So how do you respond if you receive such an invitation from a family member—or for that matter, a close friend?

This is more difficult than it may seem—or at least there are more wrinkles and angles to it. I have thought about this a great deal and have discussed it with many strong Christians. Among those I greatly respect, there is curiously a good bit of differing opinion here and I can understand and respect most of these convictions. Some would give a flat-out no to any and all such invitations. While I understand and respect this conviction, I take a less absolute approach, even though my convictions about what marriage is and is not are very firm.

I will try to address this point with many of these different thoughts in mind. And this should indicate that, like many issues we address in these chapters, there is a not a clear yes/no answer. But there are helpful guidelines.

1. *Who's inviting you?* Is it the nice man in accounting at work who audits your team's budget? Or is it your brother or child? You will certainly evaluate these two invitations differently, one causing you much more soul-searching than the other. For me, the person would have to be very special and meaningful to me.

2. *What kind of wedding?* Is it happening in a
   Christian church or conducted by a
   clergyman representing the church? What
   kind of church? Is it an Episcopal or
   Lutheran church that permits such
   weddings, but should know better, or a
   Unitarian church that has forever been on
   the side of whatever challenges biblical
   convention? Two related questions that
   should weigh in your decision are (1) is it
   a completely secular wedding at the
   country club, the beach, someone's
   backyard, or even city hall, and (2) is it
   actually a legal marriage or a commitment
   ceremony?

3. *Do they know your convictions*? This is an
   important aspect to this decision-making
   process. The few friends whose
   ceremonies I might attend know quite
   well how I feel about such relationships
   and ceremonies. They would not think for
   a moment that my attendance means I'm

softening on my convictions. They might even wonder why I'm attending. And if they asked me, it would give me an opportunity to explain precisely why I am there. I am not there to celebrate the relationship and the place it's moving to on this day, but because I love them and I wanted to be here today for them. This is important for them to know, as it is honest about my regard for them.

Making the Decision

So what to do after you receive the wedding invitation? First, the wedding is not just about the couple, with everyone else mere spectators. The attendees are participants as well, supporting the couple, rejoicing with them in what their new union is creating, and even in standing in solidarity with them and their joining families, agreeing to be there for the couple, as a couple, in the years to come in many ways. You are a stakeholder in their union.

So when some Christians say they cannot in good conscience attend any kind of same-sex wedding, it is not necessarily because they don't like "those darned gays and lesbians" but because of what they understand a marriage and a wedding to be. Along these lines, I could not imagine myself going to a heterosexual couple's "commitment ceremony," declaring their dedication to each other, while not seeing marriage itself as necessary. Even if I cared deeply for the couple, I simply couldn't participate in celebrating such a thing. In fact, to be honest, I'd think it was silly.

And this would not be any kind of statement about the people themselves, as hard as that might be for some to believe. Would I think my atheist friend hated me if he declined my invitation to attend my baptism next week? Such an event is a massive thing to a believer, but it would be unfair for me to expect him to come, much less make it a litmus test for the substance of his appreciation for me. It is just a matter of belief and conviction about what such ceremonies are. Hopefully, such Christians could explain these convictions to their gay or lesbian family members or friends in a gracious way and hope to have the couple *understand* even though they will not likely agree.

This is where I would stand in most situations. I certainly could not attend a wedding that was held in a church or officiated by clergy as a Christian wedding that was clearly outside of God's design and desire for marriage. I would not want to be a part of a seemingly Christian wedding that was clearly in contrast with Christian teaching, for I would not only be an audience member but a witness and supporter, which, as was explained, is exactly what the friends, family, and loved ones at a wedding are. It is a communal covenant that all are entering into, but of course, two more than anyone else. This I could not do and would have to decline.

Are there other circumstances under which I would go?

It depends, and it would relate primarily to the first question: Who are these folks and what is my heart toward them?

My main consideration would rest upon what this person meant to me and how I wanted to communicate my love for them. Add to this whether the wedding was a secular affair or of a faith tradition outside Christianity that had no authority in my life.

For me, if I was ever to attend a same-sex wedding, these would be the questions that I would have to wade through. I will be honest. I do have some friends whose weddings I would like to attend, solely because of what they mean to me. These particular friends harbor no illusions about my convictions here. But I care for them so deeply as people—and as "opponents"—that I would be willing to reach out and attend their weddings just to show them that despite our clear differences, I would like to be there for them. And knowing each of them as I do, none of them would be married in a church, so that eliminates that issue. But it would be a very rare and selective event for me.

This might seem inconsistent on my part to some people, and I understand and respect them if they do not understand. But in more than a few issues regarding friendships with our LGBT neighbors, there are areas that are not as black-and-white as we might like them to be and on which good and faithful Christians will disagree. But that should not keep us from seeking to find the best way through them that are true and authentic to our faith, and gracious and loving to our friends.

So, for me, I would need to be very motivated to attend such a wedding, and I would do so primarily out of love for the person who invited me.

As you work through your own decisions in these matters, ask a number of Christians whose maturity and discernment you trust. Determine what is wise in their advice and apply it to your particular situation. Of course, give it a great deal of prayer.

However, in terms of a hard line, I would say that a same-sex church wedding is something a Christian cannot participate in.

Article used by permission.

Article 3

Question: "Should a Christian attend the wedding of a gay couple?"[4]

Crosswalk.com

Answer: First, a word of encouragement: if you are the kind of friend that a gay couple would invite to their wedding, then you are probably doing something right. When Jesus ministered, those who were despised by society, the tax collectors and the sinners, drew near to Him (Matthew 9:10; Luke 15:1). He was a friend to them.

Further, no one sin is greater than another. All sin is offensive to God. Homosexuality is just one of many sins listed in 1 Corinthians 6:9–10 that will keep a person from the kingdom of God. We all sin and fall short of God's glory (Romans 3:23). It is only through Jesus Christ that we may be saved from sin's eternal consequences. (Please see *What does it mean that Jesus saves?*)

Some would contend that a Christian should have no qualms about attending a gay wedding and that one's presence at a gay wedding does not necessarily indicate support for the homosexual lifestyle. Rather, they view it as extending Christ's love toward a friend. The thought is that one's presence at a wedding ceremony is an act of love and friendship toward the person—not toward the lifestyle or spiritual choices. We do not hesitate to support friends and loved ones who struggle with other sins. Showing support and unconditional love could open doors of opportunity in the future.

The problem is that a gay wedding is a celebration of two people who are living a lifestyle that God declares to be immoral and unnatural (Romans 1:26-27). "Marriage should be honored by all" (Hebrews 13:4), but a gay wedding dishonors marriage by perverting its meaning. Unlike weddings of those in other faiths, a gay wedding does not qualify as a marriage, according to what God declares marriage to be. A marriage between a non-Christian man and non-Christian woman is still a marriage in God's eyes. It is still a fulfillment of the "one flesh" relationship that God intends (Genesis 2:24). Even a marriage between a believer and an unbeliever is a valid marriage (1 Corinthians 7:14), even though God commands believers to avoid such marriages (2 Corinthians 6:14).

A gay union is not a marriage in God's eyes. God ordained marriage to be between a man and a woman for a lifetime; to take that holy and blessed union and link it to something God declares to be unholy is unconscionable. How can we ask God's blessing on a union that He declares to be unnatural?

Suppose a Christian could attend a gay wedding and somehow communicate clearly that he is supporting only the individuals getting married and not their lifestyle. The individuals he is supporting are still holding an event which celebrates their immorality. There is no way around the fact that a gay wedding ceremony is a celebration of sin. We support an alcoholic friend by helping him refrain from drinking, not by going to a bar with him. We support a friend addicted to pornography by making him accountable and getting him help, not by helping organize his magazine collection or creating more hard drive space on his computer. In the same way, we support a homosexual friend by helping him out of the lifestyle, not by signing a guest book at a celebration of homosexuality. We do not truly help our

friends by attending an event where their sin
is applauded.

It is admirable to show love to a
friend. It is good to seek opportunities to
witness to and show kindness and love to our
gay friends. However, such motivations are
misguided when it comes to attending a gay
wedding. It is never our goal to drive our
friends away from Christ, but Christians have
a responsibility to stand up for righteousness,
even if it results in pain, division, or hatred
(Luke 12:51–53; John 15:18). If invited to a
gay wedding, it is our conviction that a
believer in Jesus Christ should respectfully
decline.

But, that is our conviction. A gay
wedding is not an issue the Bible explicitly
addresses. There definitely is no "you shall"
or "you shall not" in God's Word regarding
attending a gay wedding. Based on the
reasons and principles listed above, we
cannot envision a scenario in which

attending a gay wedding would be the right thing to do. If after much prayer, study of God's Word, thought, and discussion, you are led to a different conviction, we would not disparage your faith or question your commitment to Christ.

Article used by permission.

Article 4

Should I Attend the Wedding of a Gay Friend or Family Member?[5]

Peter Ould, Eve Tushnet,
Lisa Severine Nolland, Sherif Girgis

Do More Than Say 'No'

Peter Ould

All good pastoral theology begins with Jesus. The Gospels give us clear examples of how Jesus interacts with those whose lifestyles are not holy. He dines with tax collectors, hangs out with prostitutes, and dares to speak to unclean foreigners. Jesus has absolutely no problem doing things with sinners.

Based on this reasoning, then, we might conclude that Christians should have no problem attending a gay wedding, even if they do not agree with it. Jesus in his pastoral engagements hardly ever judged. Surely as God's salt and light, we are called to go among unbelievers, live with them, and pray for them through their joys and sorrows in hopes of witnessing for Christ.

But there's another perspective: Marriage is a God-given ordinance that speaks to more than just the love between two people. Biblical teaching on marriage shows us that the union of a man and woman is the icon of the union of Christ and his church. The Book of Revelation envisions the great wedding feast at the end of time, the union of the Bridegroom and his bride.

So doing marriage incorrectly is an act of idolatry. It's a rejection of both the ordinance God has given and the meaning of that ordinance. Since the gender of the participants in marriage is important, mixing those sexes up destroys the point marriage was meant to represent. How can a Christian be involved in such a thing?

Like many Christians, I find myself torn on this pressing issue. I describe my perspective as "postgay." Today, I have a wife and family. Years ago, I decided that my same-sex orientation would not define me. I refused to accept the idea that same-sex attraction validates same-sex behavior.

But my heart wants to come alongside my gay friends and celebrate the joy they have found. Jesus shared his life with deeply flawed sinners. My theologically trained head realizes that we need to make decisions based on the clear biblical witness.

Here's my answer: There were times when Jesus clearly and publicly identified sinful behavior for what it was—overturning the tables of the money changers in the temple, for example. Perhaps the most Christ like thing to do is to politely decline the wedding invite and explain why. Say "no"—but do not end the conversation there.

Reason alone is rarely sufficient to change someone's heart and head. When I allow others to look inside my marriage and family, they see the tension Christians face as they live in societies that do not conform to God's will. We must not isolate ourselves from a fallen world. In going beyond our Christian bubble, we see that ethical choices, even the ones Jesus made, aren't always as black and white as we might wish. Gospel-based relationships are everything. Attendance at a wedding? Probably not.

Peter Ould is a Church of England priest and a banking consultant based in Canterbury, UK. For eight years, his blog, An Exercise in the Fundamentals of Orthodoxy, chronicled his journey out of homosexuality.

∞

This article first appeared on http://www.gotquestions.org. Used by permission.

It's Best to Show Up
Eve Tushnet

When I became a Christian, most of my friends and family were baffled and disappointed. They could not understand why I was subjecting myself to a repressive falsehood. Sure, the church's paintings are nice, but what about the ethics?

That's why it was so moving to me that my best friend came to my baptism. She gamely let the priests shake holy water over her; she kept a wry, silent smile on her face while everybody else renounced Satan. I was under no illusion that she had changed her mind about Christianity and the church. That made her attendance more poignant, because it was a gesture purely in support of me.

I think of my baptism when I consider how Christians should respond when they are invited to gay weddings. (I've attended one same-sex wedding so far, in an Episcopal church.) People find it easier to notice judgment than acceptance. They find it especially hard to understand unconditional love. Whenever Christians can show that our love is not a reward for good behavior, we should do so.

This decision about attendance is easier for me, because I believe God calls some people to devoted, sacrificial love of another person of the same sex. Let me be clear: I don't think that that love should be expressed sexually. But some people who marry a same-sex partner are doing so out of a call to love, even though they misinterpret the nature of that love. We should support as much as we can. When a woman forgives offenses and humbly apologizes for her own wrongdoing, cares for children, listens, comforts, and learns to put others' needs above her own preferences, those are acts of love—which do not become worthless or loveless when they take place within a lesbian relationship.

Years down the line, if this person does choose to follow Christ, or live more fully within Christian ethics, will I have conducted myself in such a way that he or she would find me a trustworthy guide? Or will I have focused only on the areas where that relationship is not in line with Christian sexual discipline? Will I have acted as if I am obviously correct and the other person is just perversely following his own self-will?

Attempts by straight Christians to uphold essentials of the faith are often misunderstood as bigotry. But there is much actual bigotry out there. A decision not to attend a same-sex wedding takes place in the same universe as gay-bashing, bullying, and the long grind of contempt toward gay men and women. I am not blaming Christians for that; it's just the context in which Christian decisions will be interpreted. That context makes it even harder than it would be anyway to believe in unconditional love.

Some people may have already demonstrated enough love that their friends would understand a decision not to attend a same-sex wedding. But in most cases, I think it's best to show up.

Eve Tushnet, author of *Gay and Catholic*, blogs at Patheos.

Not in Good Conscience
Lisa Severine Nolland

M arriage is not only about one couple's relationship. It has a public dimension, and the wedding ceremony and the celebration mark this. That family and friends participate in a couple's wedding makes marriage a public matter.

So, by attending a same-sex wedding, I tacitly endorse this particular union and also endorse the notion that two women (or men) actually can get married. I cannot in good conscience go, because I cannot endorse same-sex marriage (SSM).

I love and live by the ethics of Jesus. Would Jesus be in attendance? He was a friend of tax collectors and sinners because that was how he could connect. Though unconditional, his love was not static. Beginning with acceptance, he moved into challenge, as seen with Zacchaeus. Would

Jesus have shown solidarity by collecting the odd bit of revenue? I don't think so. Jesus separated the person of Zacchaeus from his iniquitous business practice in order to redeem both.

I cannot in good conscience attend a same-sex wedding precisely because I love my gay friends and want their best. I believe all sin damages. My sin damages me as their sin damages them. How can I celebrate what I believe harms them? I would respect their friendship but would pray they realize that marriage is not what they are after or what they actually want. I would look for opportunities to point them to a better way. As Christian mystic Simone Weil once noted, "All sins are attempts to fill voids." My friends' marriage is an example.

Though some gay married couples may be exemplary in love and devotion, SSM has more ominous aspects. Do those advocating for SSM insist these couples conform to traditional marriage practices, such as sexual exclusivity and permanence? No. Mainstream SSM advocates such as sex columnist Dan Savage enthuse over so-called "monogamish marriage" (committed but sexually open).

Waiting in the wings could be polyamorous and bisexual marriages. How will people respond to wedding invitations from the excited trio? Research by sociologist Mark Regnerus indicates that "churchgoing Christians who support ssm are more likely to think . . . adultery [and] polyamory . . . are acceptable."

As a sex historian, I've tracked the sex revolution for decades. I've miscalled the timing, but otherwise my concerns generally have proved prescient.

I used to share my home and dog with a lovely gay man who had AIDS. A close bisexual friend "came out," confessing her love, fearful of my rejection. I hugged her but refused the sex. I have lived my life in friendship with many sexual-minority people and witnessed the pain and tragedy in their lives. But capitulating to their demands that we accept gay marriage is wrong-headed. And so, I would send my regrets but set up dinner for the following month.

Lisa Severine Nolland, Ph.D., convenes the Marriage, Sex, and Culture Group of Anglican Mainstream (Oxford) and is a consultant with anglicanmainstream.org.

Don't Go, But Love
Sherif Girgis

This couple doesn't despise tradition. They've just known what Dorothy Day called "the long loneliness"—that dull, gnawing ache for communion and transcendence. Our age makes people think in their bones that only sex and marriage provide the intimacy and love that sate us. But by reason and faith, Christians know what even the best pagan thinkers taught: marriage is the union apt to unfold into family life—fully committed and opposite-sex; and nonmarital sex is wrong.

So we cannot attend the ceremony. Wedding guests do not spectate. Their job is to bear witness to the couple's being married and support their commitment, which is partly sexual by definition.

Friendship isn't served by supporting what we think wrong. We must trade our safe, undiscerning love for

Christ's own—aflame with truth but also vulnerable and understated, free of smugness or distance. Then we must get on with serving our friend, now on alert for signs our love was conditional. We prove those suspicions wrong, slowly, in every interaction. We rejoice in the couple's deep mutual presence as companions and confidants in life's ups and downs. As with cohabiting opposite-sex couples, it isn't that their sacrificial love is unworthy. It's holy, which is why it's wrong to try to make it something it isn't.

Their companionship is invaluable, and disserved by attempts to foster it by sex. Noncoital sex (straight or gay), rather like premarital sex, seeks the experience of conjugal union without its full reality.

It fails to shape love by the whole truth about lover and beloved, who unite as one heart and mind but not as one flesh, toward any one bodily end encompassing and transcending them both. This matters because their sacrificial love does. We ask them to understand our read of things even if they don't share it.

We don't judge their hearts and can't rush persuasion in a decades-long cultural revolution. But we should have the confidence of happy counterrevolutionaries, keen to add vivid, splendid color to postmodernity's monochrome moral vision.

Many take for granted the sexual shibboleths of the industrialized West: sex simply pleases and forges felt bonds; marriage is the only realm for real love. But we have the moral vision of millennia and thinkers from East and West. Sex is an exchange of whole persons, trembling with meaning; joining man to woman as one flesh and generations as one blood. Marriage has no monopoly on love. There's a rich horizon of vocations to love, each with its own values.

Where other responsibilities allow, let us prove the promise of platonic intimacy by drawing our friends in. Not because they need us, but because we each need the other. Not to work on them, but as Montaigne said of loving his friend, and as Christ loves us: "Because it was he, because it was I."

Sherif Girgis, who is pursuing degrees at Yale and Princeton, co-wrote *What Is Marriage? Man and Woman: A Defense*, and contributes to thepublicdiscourse.com.

∞

This article first appeared in the March 17, 2015 issue of *Christianity Today*. Used by permission of *Christianity Today*, Carol Stream, IL 60188.

Article 5

Attend Your Child's Same-sex Wedding Ceremony

National Association of Evangelicals[6]

One year ago, the U.S. Supreme Court changed the legal definition of marriage to include same-sex couples. American Christians are beginning to grapple with practical and ethical questions from this decision, such as "Should I attend my child's same-sex wedding ceremony?", as they seek to live faith.

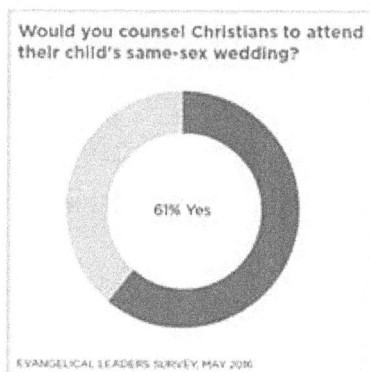

Would you counsel Christians to attend their child's same-sex wedding?

61% Yes

EVANGELICAL LEADERS SURVEY, MAY 2016

The National Association of Evangelicals (NAE) put this question to its leaders in the May Evangelical Leaders Survey. The majority of evangelical leaders (61 percent) would counsel Christians to attend their child's same-sex wedding ceremony.

"Protecting and maintaining the parent-child relationship drives the responses to this survey," said Leith Anderson, NAE president. "The values evangelical leaders hold in tension — though there are different ways of expressing them — are communicating a biblical view of marriage and showing unconditional love. Upholding both grace and truth."

Jay Barnes, president of Bethel University, advises attending the wedding. "Maintaining the relationship is vital and provides the best chance for change over time," he said.

Likewise, William Bohline, founding pastor of Hosanna! Church in Lakeville, Minnesota, said, "Presence at the wedding expresses unconditional love. Jesus showed us that that is the only power that transforms the human heart. While there might be heartache at the wedding, non-attendance only adds more mortar to the wall of separation."

One issue for many evangelical leaders is whether attending the ceremony implies endorsement of the union, with some suggesting that clear communication may provide more liberty to attend.

"Failing to attend is something you can never undo, and while I recognize that it may appear that you are giving your blessing by your presence, you can set the parameters of your participation with the couple," said Carmen Fowler LaBerge, president of Presbyterian Lay Committee.

She suggests sharing the biblical understanding of marriage privately with the couple and giving them an opportunity to share how their understanding differs. Parents can also share what kind of role they would feel comfortable with during the ceremony and surrounding events. For example, they might not want to speak a blessing, but would want to stand with the couple in their wedding party photos.

"Find what you can do without compromising your conscience or your position as parents to speak into their life at a later time should the Lord turn their heart. Don't burn a bridge that one day they might yet return across," Fowler LaBerge said. Some of those who would not advise attending a same-sex wedding ceremony urged that unconditional love be shown to the couple.

John Hopler, director of Great Commission Churches, said, "My recommendation is that a Christian respectfully and lovingly decline the invitation, but then double his or her efforts to show the love of Christ to the family member or friend in other ways."

The Evangelical Leaders Survey is a monthly poll of the Board of Directors of the National Association of Evangelicals. They include the CEOs of denominations and representatives of a broad array of evangelical organizations including missions, universities, publishers and churches.

Article used by permission.

More on The WISDOM Process©

✝ Pray

Role of Prayer

We access the guidance of God's Spirit through prayer and the Word of God. While God wants us to use our minds to study his Word to gain his revealed life direction, the Bible tells us:

> *If any of you lacks wisdom,*
> *he should ask God, who gives*
> *generously to all without finding*
> *fault, and it will be given to him.*
> —James 1:5

Bible study should be covered with prayer. Paul prayed like this for the Colossians:

> *For this reason, since the*
> *day we heard about you, we have*

> *not stopped praying for you and*
> *asking God to fill you with the*
> *knowledge of his will through all*
> *spiritual wisdom and*
> *understanding.*
>
> —Colossians 1:9

In answer to your prayers, the Spirit will shape your desires and then you will develop the mind of Christ. Rather than prayer being a specific step in The WISDOM Process©, it should be threaded throughout the process of your study from start to end.

You will find that as you pray, the Spirit of God will guide you to truth. As a group, if you will prayerfully listen to the Spirit, he will direct your conversation to deep spiritual wisdom, conviction and motivation to honor God in daily life choices.

W Work the issue: *What's really at stake*?

Prepare your heart and mind before engaging God's Word. Take a moment to pray about questions in your life and issues arising from the Scripture you are studying. Consider how the Lord may want to impact you at this time. Bring your questions to your study of God's Word.

I Investigate Scripture: *What does God say?*

God's Word is our authority for life. It is our guide for belief and behavior. Our lives must be grounded in the Word of God. It is our primary source of absolute, divine truth. Spend time prayerfully and carefully considering what the biblical text is saying.

S Seek counsel: *What do wise people say?*

After studying the Scripture for ourselves, it is wise to seek the counsel of others. In Proverbs, Solomon said there is wisdom in a multitude of counselors. Wise people listen to advice (Proverbs 12:15; 13:10; 19:20). We provide you with well-researched input in several articles to help you understand God's Word better, but of course this counsel itself must be judged by the Word of God.

D Develop your response: *What do I think?*

We learn best when we actively engage. Writing down answers to questions will deepen your interaction with God's Word. Some questions are designed to increase your focus and understanding of the Scripture; others help you extend your thinking in applying God's Word to your life.

O Openly discuss: *What do we think?*

Life transformation is increased when we sharpen each other in dynamic discussion. You will grow more if you study with a group where you can wrestle together with how to understand and obey God's Word. Together, prepared people led by the Holy Spirit will generate a dynamic in which ideas and wisdom multiply beyond what any individual could produce.

M Move to action: *What will I do?*

Christ calls us to obey all he commands (Matthew 28:20). The point of Bible study is not simply knowledge, but obedience. We are studying God's Word to be more and more conformed to the image of Jesus Christ to grow to maturity. The Bible tells us that hearing the Word without acting on it is like building a house on sand, while acting on the truth is like building a house on rock (Matthew 7:24–27; James 1:22–25). We are in the business of building houses on the Rock! Our study should lead us to move to action in the Spirit's power.

About the Author

BRUCE B. MILLER

God has given Bruce the privilege of serving as husband to his wife, Tamara, since 1983 and father to their five children. They are also blessed with their grandchildren. God used Bruce to plant Christ Fellowship in McKinney, Texas where he currently serves as senior pastor (CFhome.org). In his spare time, he loves spending time with Tamara, playing racquetball, using a chainsaw and sitting by an open fire with his chocolate Labrador, Calvin.

His passion for leadership development led to his first book, *The Leadership Baton*, written with Jeff Jones and Rowland Forman. Bruce's heart to see people live more joyful, fulfilled lives sparked the writing of *Your Life in Rhythm*, the forerunner to *Your Church in Rhythm* which applies the concepts of rhythmic living to local churches (BruceBMiller.com).

Bruce developed the innovative six-step WISDOM Process© which serves as a learning engine in the study guides for his books *Big God in a Chaotic World—A Fresh Look at Daniel, When God Makes No Sense—A Fresh Look at Habbakuk, Never the Same—A Fresh Look at the Sermon on the Mount*, and *Sexuality—Approaching Controversial Issues with Grace, Truth and Hope*.

Bruce graduated Phi Beta Kappa from the University of Texas at Austin with a B.A. in Plan II, the Honors Liberal Arts Program ('82); received a master's degree in Theology from Dallas Theological Seminary ('86); and did doctoral work at the University of Texas at Dallas in the History of Ideas (focus on philosophical hermeneutics, Hans-Georg Gadamer, and post-modernism). He taught theology for four years at Dallas Theological Seminary.

Bruce speaks and consults around the world. He founded the Centers for Church Based Training and served as Chairman of the Board for 12 years (ccbt.org).

You can follow Bruce on:

Facebook

(https://www.facebook.com/BruceBMillerAuthor)

To invite Bruce to speak, contact him at:

Website (BruceBMiller.com)

Other Resources

The publishing ministry of Dadlin ministries—an organization committed to helping people develop wisdom for life.

Dadlin Media
── *wisdom for life* ──

Resources by **Bruce B. Miller:**

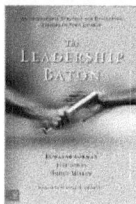

The Leadership Baton
Equips you with a solution to the need for quality leaders in local churches. Miller provides you with a biblical vision, a holistic approach and a comprehensive plan.

Your Life in Rhythm
Offers a realistic way to overcome our crazy, overly busy, stressed lives. Exposes the myth of living a "balanced" life. Miller presents "rhythmic living" as a new paradigm for relieving guilt and stress, so we can accomplish more of what matters most in life—with more freedom, peace, fulfillment and hope.

Your Church in Rhythm
Most pastors try to do everything at once, and they feel guilty if even one aspect of their church ministry is neglected in the process. Instead, Miller proposes replacing this exhausting notion of "balance" with the true-to-life concept of

"rhythm." Churches, just like people, should focus on the seasons and the cycles of ministry programs. That way, leaders can avoid burnout by focusing only on each issue at the time that it matters most.

Big God in a Chaotic World—A Fresh Look at Daniel
Shows we can live faithfully in this sinful, out-of-control world when we get a fresh vision of our big God. Daniel opens our eyes to see the God who is bigger than the problems in our world, bigger than all our fears, fires and lions.

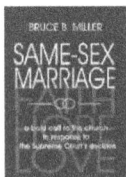

Same-Sex Marriage—A Bold Call to the Church in Response to the Supreme Court's Decision

In response to this cultural crisis, the church should step up with a Christlike response that stuns the world, and draws people to Jesus Christ with counter-cultural love.

Sexuality—Approaching Controversial Issues with Grace, Truth and Hope
Addresses the purposes of sex in marriage, singleness, cohabitation, homosexuality (and more), with fresh biblical insights filled with grace.

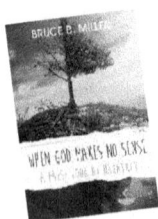

When God Makes No Sense—A Fresh Look at Habakkuk
When life is shaking you like a leaf in a storm, learn how to hold on to the unshakeable God who controls the storm.

Never the Same—A Fresh Look at the Sermon on the Mount
Explores deeper meaning in familiar lines from history's most influential speech. If we follow the spiritual kingdom vision Jesus presents, we will stand out as bright lights in this dark world, stand up when storms come and step up to receive God's eternal reward.

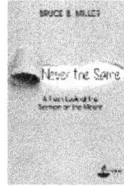

For more information on current and upcoming books, go to BruceBMiller.com.

http//brucebmiller.com_MyStory

Dadlin Media
wisdom for life

Endnotes

1. Lewis B. Smedes, *Sex for Christians: The Limits and Liberties of Sexual Living* (Grand Rapids: Eerdmans, 1976, 1994).

2. Sean McDowell and John Stonestreet, *Same-Sex Marriage (Thoughtful Response): A Thoughtful Approach to God's Design for Marriage* (Grand Rapids: Baker Books, a division of Baker Publishing Group, 2014). Used by permission. See also Adam Barr, Ron Citlau, and Kevin DeYoung, *Compassion without Compromise: How the Gospel frees us to love our gay friends without losing the truth* (Minneapolis: Bethany House, 2014).

3. Glenn T. Stanton, *Loving My (LGBT) Neighbor: Being Friends in Grace and Truth* (Chicago: Moody Press, 2014).

4. http://www.gotquestions.org/gay-wedding.html.

5. Peter Ould, Eve Tushnet, Lisa Severine Nolland, Sherif Girgis, *Should I Attend the Wedding of a Gay Friend or Family Member?* (Carol Stream, IL: Christianity Today, March 17, 2015) http://www.christianitytoday.com/ct/2015/march/gay-wedding-attend-christian-marriage-family.html.

6. *Attend Your Child's Same-sex Wedding Ceremony* (Washington, DC: National Association of Evangelicals, May 2016) https://www.nae.net/attend-childs-sex-wedding-ceremony/.